Bockarie Sama Banya

The Relationship between Simple Employee Recognition and Employee Productivity in Business Organizations

A Case Study

Anchor Academic
Publishing

Banya, Bockarie Sama: The Relationship between Simple Employee Recognition and Employee Productivity in Business Organizations. A Case Study, Hamburg, Anchor Academic Publishing 2017

Buch-ISBN: 978-3-96067-159-6
PDF-eBook-ISBN: 978-3-96067-659-1
Druck/Herstellung: Anchor Academic Publishing, Hamburg, 2017

Bibliografische Information der Deutschen Nationalbibliothek:
Die Deutsche Nationalbibliothek verzeichnet diese Publikation in der Deutschen Nationalbibliografie; detaillierte bibliografische Daten sind im Internet über http://dnb.d-nb.de abrufbar.

Bibliographical Information of the German National Library:
The German National Library lists this publication in the German National Bibliography. Detailed bibliographic data can be found at: http://dnb.d-nb.de

© Anchor Academic Publishing, Imprint der Diplomica Verlag GmbH
Hermannstal 119k, 22119 Hamburg
http://www.diplomica-verlag.de, Hamburg 2017
Printed in Germany

ABSTRACT

Some managers shy away from implementing employee recognition programs fearing high associated costs yet there are some simple and free-cost recognition programs like saying "thank you" and "well done" which are crucial like Perks.com (2012) which reported that "thank you" is a simple gesture that can make an enormous impact on any organization. It was upon this basis that the study's main purpose was to assess the relationship between simple employee recognition and employee productivity. This was guided by objectives; how best employee productivity can be determined and measured, forms of simple employee recognition, relationship between simple employee recognition and employee productivity, and strategies of how to improve employee productivity through recognition.

Related literature was reviewed and gaps regarding the level of how business organizations are embracing simple employee recognition programs and how as to what extent simple employee recognition programs relate to employee productivity. Not all companies had embraced similar recognition programs and their effect seemed to be unclear as per reviewed related literature and thus a need to fill the gap by establishing a clear relationship between simple recognition programs and employee productivity in business organizations.

A case study research design in support of both quantitative and qualitative techniques was applied, for data collection, presentation and analysis. A sample size of 400 respondents was selected and used with composition of all levels of management for M-Nic CRC. Data collection was done using questionnaires and interviews, then later presented, analysed (using Pearson correlation of **"r"**), interpreted and discussed for conclusions and recommendations.

Research findings include: Employee productivity is highly measured basing on the amount of work done within limited prior set timeframe; Praising for good work done (*r = 0.888*) and saying thank you (*r = 0.829*) are best forms of employee recognition; Simple employee recognition programs contribute positively towards achievement of improved employee productivity especially with saying thank you justified by *83%*; and Creation of goals/plans for employee recognition programs with employee involvement was highly recommended.

Study Recommendations include: Provision of good ambiance and friendly working conditions; respecting breaks and offering special holiday days; Improved and strong supervisor-employee relationship; and Keeping promises, timely feedback and respect.

DEDICATION

I dedicate this piece of work to my lovely wife Princess and to the almighty Allah.

ACKNOWLEDGMENTS

Praise is to The Almighty Allah, The Most Gracious and Provident, for The Wisdom and advancing me in knowledge to produce this manuscript.

My deep gratitude goes to Dr David Newton who laboured all day long guiding me through the research process.

My heartfelt gratitude goes to my beautiful and very supportive wife Princess.

I am very indebted to my children and best friends Rashidhatu and Iaisha.

Finally, thanks to my lovely mum Hawa and Mother in law Saphiatu.

TABLE OF CONTENTS

LIST OF TABLES

LIST OF FIGURES

ABBREVIATIONS

%	Percentage
CVI	Content Validity Index
Freq	Frequency
M-Nic CRC	M-Nic Consultancy and Research Centre Ltd
r	Pearson Correlation
SPSS	Statistical Package for Social Scientists

CHAPTER ONE: INTRODUCTION

1.1 Background to the Study

Employee recognition programs or awards according to Bonser (2013) are program activities or gifts presented to staff or volunteers as a sign of gratitude. Employee recognition is a judgment on a worker's contribution, in terms of the work process as well as dedication and motivation (Chaire, et al., 2010). Brandenberg (2013) concurs with Bonser (2013) that the reasons for receiving a recognition award include working with a company for a specific time period, completing a significant task or project, reaching a goal or selling a significant amount of products or services. In respect to the aforementioned definitions, the study focused on simple recognition in form of less costly forms of employee recognition (like saying thank you, well done, verbal appreciation, etc) and non-financial employee recognition forms (like gifts, cards, photos, end-of-year parties, offering flexible, holiday schedules, etc) plus less of or with little attention on financial employee recognition forms (like bonuses, salary increments, etc).

Some employers spend hundreds of dollars (invest heavily) on recognition programs or awards; however, this is not necessary as there are other cheap or less costly simple forms of employee recognition systems which the study focused on. Balle (2013) added that non-financial simple employee recognition programs are cheap to implement and thus important for any business organization with employee motivation problem. Frost (2014) is in agreement Balle (2013) as she emphasised that employee recognition activities do not require a large investment and many simple and yet free or cheap recognition ideas keep employees happy and fulfilled as compared to financial oriented recognition systems.

Laura (2010) defined employee productivity or equally termed as labour productivity to be concerned with the amount (volume) of output that is obtained from each employee. Muhammed (2011) and Bloch (2014) concurred on the definition of employee/labour productivity as the Units of output per labour hour or units of output per shift. De-Koninck & Griego (2000) equally defined employee productivity as how much an employee accomplishes in a certain amount of time.

Globally, 9 out of 10 now invest in employee recognition (Aviva, 2011). This means that employee recognition is embraced worldwide. Giving regular praise and recognition is essential in any organization, large or small, and will aid performance, teamwork, retention and overall employee engagement. Caon (2012) reported in 2012 that Siemens UK won an award for employee recognition. According to Aviva (2011), over 55% of employees in UK strongly agree that the quality of their companies recognition programme impacts their job performance; 80% of UK respondents feel that recognition programmes strengthen relationships with employers; 42% of employees in UK consider a company's reward and recognition programme when seeking employment.

Irvine (2012) equally reported that employee recognition is among the six essentials the employee wants in their job in South Africa, Asia or Pacific region and usually specifically about China. Atambo et al., (2013) greatly attributed employee recognition in form of incentives play a key role in enhancing performance or productivity at both individual and organizational levels in Kenya and across East Africa

Not only that employee recognition is embraced internationally like in UK (Aviva, 2011) and China (Irvine, 2012), African wise like in South Africa (Irvine, 2012), and in east African region like in Kenya (Atambo, et al., 2013), but also, employee recognition has been traced among Ugandan business organizations like MTN Uganda and M-Nic Consultancy & Research Centre (Ntabgoba, 2013). MTN Uganda on 22nd February 2013 announced and recognised the winners of the 2012 Y'ello Stars program, which is a peer to peer initiative within the MTN group meant to recognise and reward employees who are outstanding in performance, based on set parameters and as the MTN's biggest and most prestigious recognition programme to help drive and encourage performance and excellence through recognition by peers and leaders in Africa, the Middle East and generally in all 21 countries where MTN operates (Ntabgoba & Sekadde, 2013).

Irvine (2012) cautioned that despite employee recognition being beneficial to every business organization, there are associated costs especially with financial employee recognition programs or costs of poor decision making and poor implementation of employee recognition programs. This is contrary to Cavanaugh (2014) who absolutely observed that employee recognition is designed to create a better working environment that would enable employees improve their productivity and in line with (Brandenberg, 2013) and Andy Smith (2010) who observed that a mere "thank you" motivates employees to do their best on a daily basis through improving their employee productivity, and simple employee recognition is essential to the morale of every workplace which consequently have a positive impact on their productivity respectively.

This implies that most organizations should be treasuring employee recognition which is not the case and more so, not all organizations that embrace employee recognition have benefited from improved employee productivity (Irvine, 2012). Therefore, the question remains as to whether specifically simple employee recognition programs improve employee productivity in reference to M-Nic Consultancy & Research Centre, as one the prior highlighted business firms that embrace employee recognition in Uganda.

1.2 Problem Statement

There are still contrasting views or gaps regarding the factors attributable to improved employee productivity. For instance, employee recognition has been criticized for its associated costly expenses with Irvine (2012) cautioning that *"Stressed organizations could be in danger of making employee reward decisions that they come to regret if they abandon too readily the principles that underpin their people strategies."* On the other hand, it has been established that measuring and improving employee performance based on productivity is a key strategy for enhancing organizational success through improved performance (Andy, 2010; Bennett, 2014). Among other associated benefits accruing from treasuring and implementing employee recognition programs; maximizing employee productivity involves employee recognition (Slusher, 2010), simple employee recognition is an essential component to the morale of every workplace (Andy, 2010), and keeping morale high through employee recognition programs increases productivity (Frost, 2014). Despite all the numerous benefits associated with employee recognition, some of the business organizations are failing to formally embrace employee recognition even with the cheap or free or less costly simple employee recognition programs like saying "thank you", photograph of employee of the month at the reception, appreciation card, and saying "well done". It is pursuant to the forgone that the researcher set out with the intent to critically examine the relationship between simple employee recognition and employee productivity.

1.3 Purpose of the Study

The purpose of this study was to critically analyse the relationship between Simple Employee Recognition and Employee Productivity in Business Organizations. A case study of M-Nic Consultancy and Research Centre Ltd (CRC Ltd).

1.4 Objectives of the Study

i. To assess how best employee productivity can be determined and measured in business organizations

ii. To critically assess various forms of simple employee recognition programs used in business organizations

iii. To analyze the relationship between simple employee recognition and employee productivity in business organizations

iv. To establish strategies of how to improve employee productivity through simple employee recognition programs

1.5 Research Questions

i. How best employee productivity can be determined and measured in business organizations?

ii. What are the various forms of simple employee recognition programs used in business organizations

iii. What is the relationship between simple employee recognition and employee productivity in business organizations

iv. What strategies can be employed in business organizations to improve employee productivity through simple employee recognition programs

1.6 Significance and Observable Outcomes from the study

Organizations: Study findings revealed the secrets behind simple employee recognition and in particular, help business organizations such as M-Nic CRC to believe whether or not recognition of employees` work done increases satisfaction and productivity.

Managers: The study further uncovered human behavior in terms of recognition programs at the work place, like increased productivity as a result of saying thank you and showing appreciation to employees for their work done. In order words how well managers acknowledge or reward their staff as a result of good performance.

Future researchers: The study would be of great use to the researchers in the field of management since it will act as reference of different citations in their respective studies.

4

The researcher: The study became the source of knowledge and skills to the researcher, in terms of gaining full knowledge and practical experience in research methods (how to conduct a research study), in addition to understanding the relationship between simple employee recognition and employee productivity in the practical sense. The study also helped to broaden the horizon of the research in the area of management especially as it relates to performance management.

1.7 Research Structure

The study was presented and structured in five (5) chapters as briefly elucidated below:

The first chapter deals with introduction and thus entailing; background to the study, problem statement, purpose of the study, study specific objectives, research questions, and significance of the study in addition to observable outcomes from the study.

The second chapter covered review of the related literature in accordance with the study objectives which included; how best employee productivity can be determined and measured, forms of simple employee recognition programs, relationship between simple employee recognition and employee productivity, and strategies of how best managers and employers can improve employee productivity through simple employee recognition programs.

The third chapter goes further to elaborate the methodology adopted in the form of; research design, study population, sample size and composition, sampling strategy, data sources, data collection methods, data quality control, data collection procedure, data presentation and analysis, study limitations and way-forward to the limitations.

The fourth chapter describes how data was presented, how data was interpreted and how the presented data was analysed. Furthermore, discussions centred around major findings was done under chapter four. This was done in accordance with the study objectives and as per the stipulated methodology.

The fifth chapter expound on the presented study findings in the form of; summary of key findings from the related literature, summary of key findings from the primary research, main conclusions from the combined findings of literature and primary research, recommendations to the study and suggested areas for future research.

CHAPTER TWO: LITERATURE REVIEW

2.1 Introduction

This chapter provides detailed explanations of the topic under study in relation to the study objectives. These explanations were drawn from a variety of secondary sources which include; publications, magazines, reports, textbooks, among other sources.

2.2 Conceptualization of Employee Recognition

According to Bonser (2013), employee recognition programs are series of activities or gifts presented to staff or volunteers as a sign of gratitude. Employee recognition is a judgment on a worker's contribution, in terms of the work process as well as dedication and motivation to work (Chaire, et al., 2010). However, the researcher would wish to focus on simple recognition in the shape of less costly forms of employee recognition (like saying thank you, well done, verbal appreciation, etc) and non-financial employee recognition forms (like gifts, cards, photos, end-of-year parties, offering flexible, holiday schedules, framed photograph of employee of the month at the entrance or reception, etc). Thus, financial employee recognition forms like bonuses and salary increments were less of focus as per this study.

2.3 Conceptualization of Employee Productivity

Employee or labour productivity according to a renowned scholar Laura (2010) is concerned with the amount (volume) of output that is obtained from each employee. Muhammed (2011) and Bloch (2014) also concurred on the definition of employee or labour productivity as the Units of output per labour hour or units of output per shift. De-Konink & Griego (2000) equally defined employee productivity as how much an employee accomplishes in a certain amount of time.

2.4 Theoretical Perspective of Employee Recognition and Productivity

According to Chaire, et al., (2010), there are many theoretical viewpoints on employee recognition and these have been grouped according to four main theoretical viewpoints: ethical, humanist and existential, psychodynamics of work, and behavioural approach, as illustrated below;

Figure 2.4.1: Theoretical views on employee recognition

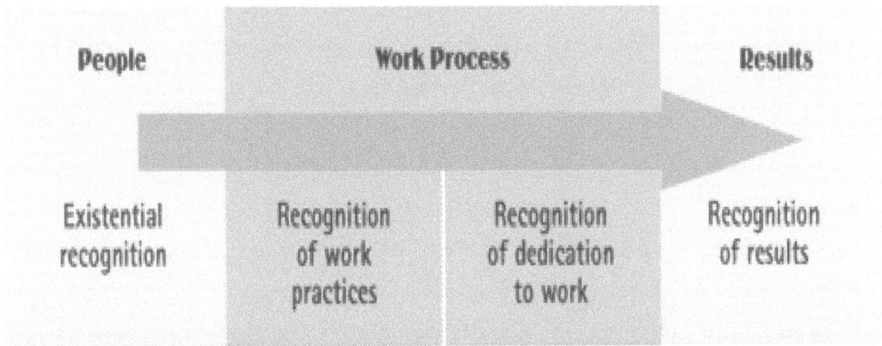

Source: Chaire, et al., (2010).

As illustrated above, the theoretical views as represented and implied are highlighted hereunder:

The ethical theoretical perspective: The ethical perspective considers human beings as dignified, equal, shared individual and collective duty to show concern for others (De-Konink, & Griego, 2000). *The humanist and existential theoretical view:* The humanist and existentialist view emphasizes human beings as fully unique and distinct, places unconditional faith in humans and their potential and recognition is perceived as special attention to a person (Chaire, et al., 2010). *The psychodynamics of work theory:* The psychodynamics of work looks at the subjective experiences of people in the workplace, and recognition is perceived as a reward experienced mainly at a symbolic level, and is given for actual work done (De-Konink & Griego, 2000). *The behavioral theoretical approach:* The behavioral approach focuses on observable and controllable individual behaviors, work results, asserts that behavior is stimulated by the resulting consequences, and ties in with the concept of contribution or reward (Chaire, et al., 2010).

2.5 How best employee productivity can be determined and measured in business organizations

According to Corbett et al., (2012), one standard measurement of productivity is output per worker- hour, or the ratio between the number of hours worked to total output – and that one can also measure productivity per week or month, if each unit of production takes more than an hour to create. However, Bloch (2014) noted that employee productivity should be measured based on tasks measurement or targets to be met not hours or days. Bennett (2014) and Bloch (2014) concurred on the point that, the metric that matters in employee productivity measurement is task completion in terms of individual or organizational set objectives or targets, not minutes or hours spent at the office.

Employee productivity should be based on breaking down the work into tasks and assigning them appropriately until projects are complete (Glascock, 2013; Bloch, 2014). According to Laura (2010), Labour productivity is concerned with the amount (volume) of output that is obtained from each employee. It is a key measure of business efficiency, particularly for firms in which the production process is labour-intensive. Based on the old adage of "You can not improve what you can't measure" Muhammed (2011) noted that employee or labour productivity or performance (in terms of productivity, efficiency and effectiveness) can be expressed as the Units of output per labour hour or units of output per shift.

It is however noted that employee productivity is measured depending on the nature of the work done by different employees at different level of management. For instance, Corbett et al., (2012) further noted that the most effective means of measuring performance by sales representatives is by taking into account and measuring each of the following factors: the volume of sales in dollars per given unit of time, the number of calls made upon existing accounts, the number of new accounts opened, and the currency amount expended per sale. Equally, Laura (2010) had earlier observed that determining the best tool for measuring productivity depends on the purposes of measurement and how the information will be used. Employee productivity measurement is best when tasks or results are used as determining factors. Measure tasks, not hours of time worked (Bennett 2014). Thanks to social media platforms and other technological developments, work and personal life continue to overlap. There are plenty of distractions throughout the day competing with different priorities, so employers have to simply ask themselves whether the needed work gets done. Breaking down tasks and crossing them off as they are completed is more helpful than having employees punch a time clock (hrcom.com, 2014). Results are the most important deciding factor of employee worth (Bennett, 2014). In essence, priority should be placed on results rather than methods.

2.6 Various forms of simple employee recognition programs used in business organizations

Many employers look for ways and meansto let their employees know that their hard work is noticed and recognized, as some plan employee appreciation days or activities to publicly recognize their top employees. (Brandenberg, 2013; Glascock, 2013). According to Brandenberg (2013), seeking ideas to let star performers know that their efforts have not gone unnoticed, an organization can choose from many different types of employee appreciation activities like extra day of paid time off in line with Laura (2010) and Martin (2014), special parking space, recognizing employee of the month with banquet of flowers or a framed poster or card expressing the company`s appreciation, morning coffees, lunch, and among others. Companies or business individuals often find themselves in a position of wanting to send thank you gifts as simple employee recognition (Bolton, 2013). Sometimes they present gifts to their own employees for a job well done; other times they want to thank clients or firms that provide business or the prospect of business. Balle (2013) and Frost (2014), it was clearly pointed out by Bolton (2013) that no-matter how large or small the company is, and likewise, no matter how large or small the token of appreciation, thanking someone for their patronage or hard work is just good business for improved employee productivity at a cheap cost.

Recognition awards as clearly put by Bonser (2013) are gifts presented to staff or volunteers as a sign of gratitude. Brandenberg (2013) equally concurs with Bonser (2013) that the reasons for receiving a recognition award include working with a company for a specific time period, completing a significant task or project, reaching a goal or selling a significant amount of products or services. Some employers spend hundreds of dollars on recognition awards; however, this is not necessary. The cost of the award is not nearly as important as the symbolism behind it. Balle (2013) added that non-financial simple employee recognition programs are cheap to implement and thus important for any business organization with employee motivation problem. Frost (2014) is in agreement Balle (2013) as she emphasised that employee recognition activities do not necessarily require a large investment and many simple and yet free or cheap recognition ideas keep employees happy and fulfilled.

Bonser et al., (2013) noted that simple employee recognition programs can take many forms; take a picture of the employee receiving her award and/or posing with her superiors (Bonser,

2013). Print the picture and have her superiors write a line or two on it, along with their signatures and a metallic pen or permanent marker works best. Place the picture in an envelope and send it to her home, or place it in her workplace mailbox, as a far more personalized and less expensive version of a thank-you card. Promotion is a very meaningful non-monetary employee recognition gift (Balle, 2013). The promotion does not have to be significant or associated with a pay rise -- it could simply be a promotion by name only. If possible, give the employee more responsibility or supervisory privileges over a person or group as a reward for his past efforts. The possibility for future promotions of this nature that will move him up the ranks may be just the push he needs to keep performing well. Bringing in gourmet coffee on Friday mornings or pay for a department breakfast or lunch once a month (Brandenberg, 2013). The actual food products or restaurants do not have to be expensive, as the main point is to let employees know that their efforts have not gone unnoticed. This breeds healthy competition among staff.

2.7 The relationship between simple employee recognition and employee productivity in business organizations

Employee recognition is designed to create a better working environment that would enable employees improve their productivity (Cavanaugh, 2014). When employees feel valued and appreciated, the workplace should see an increase in morale, job satisfaction and productivity. This implies that most organizations should be treasuring employee recognition which is not the case and more so, not all organizations that embrace employee recognition have benefited from improved employee productivity. In relation to the definition of employee recognition by Chaire, et al., (2010), measuring employee performance is a key strategy for organizational success as a result of employee motivation and improved productivity (Andy, 2010). By keeping a fair and consistent evaluation methodology, managers can determine where inefficiencies exist, identify strong employees for promotion and development and award salary increases and bonuses in a quantifiable way.

Keeping morale high through employee recognition programs increases productivity and the chances are that the organization will retain effective employees (Frost, 2014). This is contrary to the views of Andy (2010) who had observed that a big challenge in running a business towards achieving success is retaining employees as hiring and training new employees is often so expensive and time consuming. Therefore, making sure the ones who do stay are putting in productive time is important (Andy & Slusher, 2010). This was emphasized by Slusher (2010) that maximizing employee productivity the right way involves employee recognition through setting measurable goals, equipping the employees with the right tools and eliminating the negative stress tactics that lead to burnout and scattered results. Thus, greater chances of improving employee motivation and productivity.

An employee recognition program promotes a positive environment in the office (Balle, 2013). Recognizing employees shows them they are valued members of the team, employee recognition activities do not require a large investment, many simple and free recognition ideas keep employees happy and fulfilled (Balle, 2013; Frost, 2014). However, most managers have failed to formally recognize high performing employees since they connect salaries or bonuses to employment contract and culture, like as noted by Irvine (2012). *"To get everyone performing together productively, employers need to create a culture of appreciation, recognition, and reward"*. Irvine (2012) further emphasized the contribution of simple employee recognition towards improving employee productivity.

Heathfield (2004) in his study in a Gallup Poll in 2004 reported that employee recognition married together with a culture enriched rewards program deliver; 27% higher profits, 50% higher sales, and 50% higher customer loyalty. This implies that organizational culture greatly determines the extent to which simple employee recognition programs embraced by the specific organization influences positively the employees` productivity, like as supported by Bonser (2013). However, Bersin (2012) cautioned that while this sounds like a recipe for success, disaster may strike, if the program does not foster a culture aligned with the company's culture, goals and objectives.

2.8 Strategies of how to improve employee productivity through simple employee recognition programs

For improved employee productivity, holiday meals come around all year with Easter, Independence Day, Thanksgiving and Christmas (Frost, & Martin, 2014). Have a holiday meal catered at the office or a nice restaurant. Allow a longer lunch or dinner break so they can fully enjoy the experience. The point is to get your staff out of their normal lunch rut and give them a chance to enjoy themselves with other members of the staff. From a simple "thank you" to a full-fledged banquet, there are many levels of employee recognition that can continue to motivate employees to do their best on a daily basis through improving their employee productivity (Brandenberg, 2013). On the same note, Andy (2010) emphasized that simple employee recognition is essential to the morale of every workplace, and that it is a common misconception that employees need to be recognized in a grandiose way in order to feel validated. Many times a simple applauding verbal statement, a lunch or a movie pass will do the trick and guarantee they will feel appreciated for their hard work, which will consequently have a positive impact on their productivity.

Employees' ability, competency and productivity should be measured against their peers regularly (Andy, 2010). This implies that according to Andy (2010) and in line with Bennett (2014), it is helpful to both the employee and the company overall regarding employee productivity measurement through identifying areas where an employee may be trailing his colleagues, as a personal development plan can be put in place. Similarly, if a negative trend is seen among a number of employees, company controls and procedures can be evaluated to address these problems at a general level (Andy & Slusher, 2010). Simple employee recognition programs or activities can be used to motivate employees and consequently improving their employee productivity through; identifying or realizing an opportunity to praise someone (Harrison, 2008), acknowledging or recognizing employee for their good work (Harter & Killham, 2003), appreciation messages or cards (Laura, 2010; Martin, 2014), formal and informal monetary or non-monetary recognition rewards (Luciano, 2012).

2.9 Conceptual Framework

Figure 2.9.2: Conceptual Framework

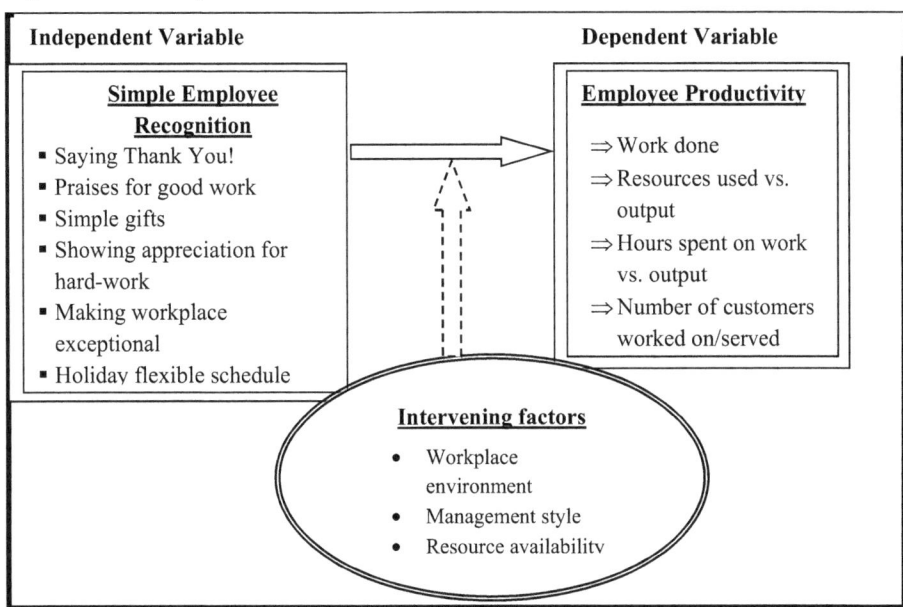

Source: Personally designed

The independent variable is represented by simple employee recognition programs that are offered by business organizations and these include "thank you or well done", showing appreciation and offering friendly working environment. These components of simple employee recognition programs (independent variable) are assumed to enable the organization achieve its objectives especially including employee productivity (dependent variable), which can be determined in form of either by amount of work-done, resources used vs. output, working hours spent vs. output or customers served. However, the dependent variable can only be achieved if other intervening factors (like workplace, management, or resources) are taken into consideration, despite independent variable.

13

CHAPTER THREE: METHODOLOGY

3.1 Introduction

In general, a deductive research approach was adopted and the focus was therefore on testing the theory (perspective theory as noted by Chaire, et al., 2010). With the application of a case study research design alongside quantitative and qualitative designs or techniques, findings generated from representative respondents were based on making the right generalisation (for inferential purposes) using correlation analysis (Pearson Correlation represented by r) to establish the relationship between simple employee recognition and employee productivity.

Research methods being the specific ways in which data is gathered within an overall strategy of research, the ways for this study were in the form of; research design, study population, sample size, sampling techniques, data sources, data collection techniques/instruments, data quality control, data presentation and analysis, limitations and delimitations to the study.

3.2 Research Design

In line with the reviewed related literature in accordance with the study objectives, a deductive approach was identified as the best suitable for this study as justified by observations made by different authors such as Bloch (2014) on measurement dimensions of employee productivity, Brandenberg (2013) regarding forms of simple employee recognition programs, Frost (2014) regarding employee recognition and productivity, and Andy (2010) regarding strategies for improving employee productivity through recognition.

An overall deductive research approach was used due to the fact that the study started from objectives and theoretical perspectives (testing theories) to inference logical conclusions and recommendations based on empirical findings.

A case study research design was adopted using M-Nic Consultancy & Research Centre (M-Nic CRC Ltd). With suggestion by Odiya (2009) that using mixed methodologies is better, qualitative and quantitative research approaches plus correlation analysis research technique was also applied to that end. The basic reason for the use of case study research design was that it could enable the researcher to study a group in details so as to make generalization based on group detailed findings regarding simple employee recognition and productivity. Basic reason for the use of quantitative and qualitative in tandem with correlation research

14

techniques was that they help to collect data which was presented, analysed and processed using statistical or mathematical methods and descriptive or narrative methods respectively – in a bid to establish a correlational relationship between study variables of simple employee recognition and productivity.

3.3 Study Population and Sample size

Most of authors as revealed by the many reviewed related literature noted varying views regarding relationship between simple employee recognition and employee productivity like Andy (2010) and Cavanaugh (2014). This implied that first-hand information often needed to be obtained and thus adoption of a case study research design which required establishment of study population for which a representative sample was selected.

Population of the study was 995, which included all levels of management and ordinary employees of M-Nic Consultancy & Research Centre (M-Nic CRC). A sample size of 400 respondents was chosen and was specifically composed of 8 top officials, 32 middle managers, 90 lower managers/supervisors, and 270 ordinary employees of M-Nic CRC.
The following formula was used for sample size determination (Krycee & Morgan, 1970).

$$\text{Sample size (n)} = \frac{N}{1 + N\,(e)^2}$$

n = Sample size; N = Population size; e = Level of precision (0.05)

For instance, determining sample size (n) for ordinary employees;

$$\Rightarrow \frac{832}{1 + 832\,(0.05)^2} = \frac{832}{1 + 2.08} = \underline{\mathbf{270}}$$

Table 3.3.1: Sample size and composition

Respondent Category	Population (N)	Sample Size (n) $=\dfrac{N}{1 + N\,(e)^2}$	Sampling Strategy
Top management	8	8	Simple random
Middle management	35	32	Simple random
Lower management	116	90	Stratified sampling
Ordinary employees	832	270	Stratified sampling
Total	**995**	**400**	

Source: Krycee & Morgan (1970)

3.4 Sampling Technique

The study employed stratified sampling method to categorize respondents according to their levels of management in terms of top management, middle management, and lower management including ordinary employees. This follows the fact that the sample representative of the study population needs to be appropriate and objective (from all categories of respondents) like as noted by Corbett & Marcia (2012) in chapter two of the related literature review, that, *"employee productivity is measured depending on the nature of the work done by different employees at different level of management"*.

Lottery method of simple random was applied to randomly select required numbers from each of management level stratum, due to the fact the method gave equal chances to all and it enabled all members of the population to be given numbers that are written on small pieces of paper. If we are to follow Sekaran' (2003) advice, which involved pieces of paper being folded, put in a bag or basket, carefully shuffled and then drawn one at a time until the required number of respondents was obtained. The main reason for use of lottery method was that all lower managers and ordinary employees required equal treatment, and thus, they were having equal chances of being picked at any selection point.

3.5 Data Sources

3.5.1 Primary data

In addition to the review of the related literature for already existing information, first-hand information was presumed the most appropriate for empirical findings and as indirectly suggested by Corbett & Marcia (2012).

Therefore, the primary sources of data were inclusive of the researcher going to the branches of M-Nic Consultancy & Research Centre (M-Nic CRC) across the country, and gathered first-hand information using open-ended and closed-ended questionnaires as subjected to all categories of respondents and face-to-face interviews with only key informants.

3.5.2 Secondary data

The secondary sources of data as the already existing information was obtained by reviewing related literature guided by the study`s specific objectives and the main purpose of the study, like as presented under chapter two for literature review from different authors.

Therefore, secondary data were inclusive of the researcher visiting public libraries, university libraries, plus taking advantage of other data sources such as Newspapers, Textbooks, Journals (like that of De-Konink & Griego, 2000), and Internet like information from (Frost, Cavanaugh, & Martin, 2014).

3.6 Data Collection Methods and Instruments

3.6.1 Guided Interviews

Managers as very key informants were subjected to face-to-face interviews, for the purposes of gathering information on a person to person basis where deeper probing was needed to supplement data collected using questionnaires on simple recognition programs and productivity. Interviews were required as crucial, to additionally prove some authors' views like that of Frost (2014), that, *"keeping morale high through employee recognition programs increases productivity"*.

Interview questions were derived from the study objectives and the structure of the interview questions were based on the different views of authors especially Irvine (2012) and Andy (2010) or Cavanaugh (2014) who had differing views on the relationship between simple employee recognition and employee productivity. More basic reasons behind the use of interviews included; a need to obtain detailed information from interviewees through paraphrasing questions or re-asking interviewees which cannot be achieved under other data collection methods, a great need to obtain vital and confidential information which may not necessarily be obtained through questionnaire method, enabling probing for confirmations and clarifications for justified, explained and unbiased information.

3.6.2 Questionnaire

Well-designed open-ended and closed-ended questionnaires were main data collection tools, which involved a set of questions as stipulated in the study objectives and to facilitate critical reviews. The design and structuring of questions were mainly driven by the content of study objectives in line with existing information as per the literature review. For instance, capturing the following optional views under the objective two regarding various forms of simple employee recognition programs; "saying thank you to employees" by Heathfield (2004) or Bersin (2012) and "offering simple gifts to employees" by Harter & Killham (2003).

Therefore, respondents had alternative choices (in accordance with literature review as highlighted by different authors' views) regarding closed ended questions following guidance of Sekaran (2003) and equally open-ended questions for briefly explained responses. More basic reasons behind use of such structured questionnaire (method) included; to achieve convenience during data collection on the side of respondents and thus increasing chances of obtaining responses from many respondents (for high response rate), to limit respondents for responses within the scope as per objectives and for comparative purposes with the existing literature, to avoid interview bias due to direct personal interactions with interviewees, and to minimise time (for time saving purposes) as questionnaires can be administered and collected from the respondents together with (or alongside) work compilation.

3.6.3 Documentary Literature

The available relevant reports and documents were reviewed, which included among others; Board of Directors meeting minutes, corporate governance reports, audited reports, and field reports. For comparison purposes with the existing related literature, more concrete secondary information was obtained in order to support first-hand information, as required under the adopted deductive overall research approach. More basic reasons for documentary literature were but not limited to the following; to empirically supplement questionnaire and interview findings, to obtain necessary and essential information at less cost, and to facilitate collection of factual information from reliable data sources as the ones advised by Odiya (2009).

3.7 Measurements of Variables

The appropriate measurements adopted and used were categorized in an orderly form using the Four Likert Scale, as shown below. Measurement of variables formed the basis of research information regarding the extent of individual differences on a given variable (Saunders, et al., 2003). Not only that, measurement of variables using a likert scale for varying degrees followed the fact that different authors as espoused in the literature review had differing views on simple employee recognition and productivity like the positive views of Andy (2010); Bennett (2014); and Cavanaugh (2014), contrary to the negative views of Irvine (2012) regarding the relationship between simple employee recognition and productivity of employees.

4	3	2	1
Strongly agree	Agree	Disagree	Strongly disagree

3.8 Validity and Reliability

3.8.1 Validity of Instruments
The validity of an instrument refers to the ability of the instrument to collect justifiable and truthful data, thus, ability of the instrument to measure what it is developed to measure (Sekaran, 2003; Odiya, 2009). Content related validity was based on the establishing of validity of instruments by use of two raters who were experts in the study field of employee recognition and productivity. Raters were used and they enabled the researcher to evaluate instrumental content to determine whether they covered all study aspects.

The CV formula is: $CVI = \dfrac{\text{Number of items (questions) rated as relevant}}{\text{Total number of items in Questionnaire}}$

CVI of 0.9 (90%) was considered valid since it was greater than 0.7 (70%), as the benchmark percentage for CVI in which the data collection instrument is presumed to yield valid and reliable data.

3.8.2 Reliability of Information.
Reliability of an instrument refers to the ability of the instrument to collect the same data consistently under similar conditions, thus, accuracy and consistency of collected data (Odiya, 2009). Test-retest reliability was used and this was aimed at collection of relevant data about study variables from management and employees of M-Nic CRC by use of the same instrument on two different well specified occasions. Participant`s scores were recorded on the two administering occasions and correlation between them was later calculated. The correlation coefficient became the measure of test-retest reliability, and the value of 90% was obtained and this was ok since it was greater than the normal standard percentage of 70% in which it can be considered good for research purposes.

3.9 Data Presentation and Analysis
Collected data was presented using frequency and percentage tables and figures. The researcher used descriptive analysis, which involved editing, coding and classification. Data from the filled questionnaires was then processed in such a way that it could be entered into the computer for further analysis which was later worked on using SPSS package (due to many data analysis components like Pearson`s Correlation represented by **"r"** which the

study embraced). This proved right some authors` views regarding simple employee recognition and employee productivity like Heathfield (2004) in his study in a Gallup Poll in 2004 who reported that employee recognition deliver; 27% higher profits, 50% higher sales, and 50% higher customer loyalty due to improved employee satisfaction and productivity.

3.10 Ethical Implication

In line with most of the researchers like Sekaran (2003) and Odiya (2009), researchers are supposed to restrict their activities to practices that are ethically sound. All work and correspondences were treated with secrecy and confidentiality they deserved. This was why instruments like questionnaires were bearing no names. Respondents and their views were highly respected, and there were no falsification of data or information. Dissertation Approval and Ethics Sign-off Form was completed alongside obtaining a consent letter from M-Nic CRC, in line with the University`s Dissertation Ethical Requirements.

3.11 Limitation to the Study and Solutions to the Limitations

- The researcher was expected to have limited time due to the fact that a lot of work to be accomplished was required in a very limited time.

  However, the researcher endeavoured to be good time manager especially during data collection and successfully overcame the expected time constraint.

- Respondents most of whom were expected to fail or delay to fill the questionnaires given to them or become reluctant to give vital information.

  To mitigate that, the researcher however obtained telephone contacts of all respondents and communicated effectively which yielded effective questionnaire administration and successfully gathered sufficient and reliable data.

- Some respondents answered using short forms and wrote vaguely, which somehow became hard to understand.

  To overcome such a hurdle the researcher had to notify and had kindly requested respondents when distributing questionnaires over the use of short forms and this minimised the problems that would have surfaced. He further first perused through the collected questionnaires and obtained clarification s from respondents on vague answers and short-form words before leaving the field.

CHAPTER FOUR: DATA PRESENTATION, ANALYSIS, INTERPRETATION, AND DISCUSSION OF STUDY FINDINGS

4.1 Introduction

This chapter entails presentation of the relationship between simple employee recognition and employee productivity in business organizations in Uganda, a case study of M-Nic CRC Ltd. It further entails the analysis, interpretation, and discussion of study findings regarding specific objectives; to find out how best employee productivity can be determined and measured in business organizations, to identify various forms of simple employee recognition programs used in business organizations, to examine the relationship between simple employee recognition and employee productivity, and to establish strategies of how to improve employee productivity through simple employee recognition programs.

4.2 General Information

The dissertation covered the general information on respondents and these included; sex for the respondents, age, level of education, category of respondents and work experience for all the respondents. This justified the relevance and reliability of data collected from the selected respondents. Findings regarding respondents' general information include;

Table 4.2.2: Gender of respondents

Sex of respondents	Frequency	Percentage (%)
Male	155	39%
Female	245	61%
Total	**400**	**100%**

Source: Primary Data

As presented in the table 4.2.2 above, 39% of the respondents were males and 61% of the respondents were females. This shows that M-Nic CRC employs more female workers than males, like as noted from the firm's human resource records which indicated 577 female employees (58%) and 418 male employees (42%). Thus the biggest number of M-Nic CRC workers who had relevant and reliable information were more of females than males, as selected and involved by the researcher.

21

Table 4.2.3: Age of respondents

Age in years	Frequency	Percentage (%)
Below 20 years	0	0%
20 – 30 years	180	45%
31 – 40 years	160	40%
41 years & beyond	60	15%
Total	**400**	**100%**

Source: Primary Data

As shown from table 4.2.3 above, 45% of the respondents were in the age bracket of 20 to 30 years of age, 40% of the respondents were in the age bracket of 31 to 40 years of age, and 15% of the respondents were 41 years and beyond. This implies that most of the respondents were mature enough (above 20 years of age) to understand and relate issues of simple employee recognition to employee's productivity.

Table 4.2.4: Level of Education

Educational level (qualification)	Frequency	Percentage (%)
Secondary & below	25	6%
Certificate/Diploma	95	24%
Bachelor's Degree	263	66%
Masters & PhD	17	4%
Total	**400**	**100%**

Source: Primary Data

As seen from table 4.2.4 above, it can be seen that 6% of the respondents had reached secondary level of education and primary level of education, 24% of the respondents were certificate and diploma holders, 66% of the respondents were holders of degrees, and 4% were holders of Master degree and PhD. This means that the biggest percentage of respondents were highly educated with University's bachelor's degree and thus ability for all respondents to understand English or wordings used for questionnaires without much influence.

Table 4.2.5: Category of respondents

Respondent category	Frequency	Percentage (%)
Top management level	8	2%
Middle management	32	8%
Lower management	90	23%
Ordinary employees	270	67%
Total	**400**	**100%**

Source: Primary Data

As presented from table 4.2.5 above, 2% of the respondents were representing the company's top management level, 8% of the respondents were representing middle management level, 23% of the respondents were representing lower management level including the supervisors, and 67% of the respondents were representing ordinary workers. All management and staff of M-Nic CRC got a chance to participate in the study and this can be seen in the fact that most of the respondents were ordinary workers due to their large population.

Table 4.2.6: Working experience of respondents

Working experience in years	Frequency	Percentage (%)
Less than 1 year	85	21%
1 – 3 years	105	26%
4 years & above	210	53%
Total	**400**	**100%**

Source: Primary Data

From the above table 4.2.6 of the research findings, 21% of the respondents had worked with M-Nic CRC for a period of less than one (1) year, 26% of the respondents had a working experience with M-Nic CRC of 1 to 3 years, and 53% of the respondents had working experience with M-Nic CRC for a period of 4 year and above. This can be seen that most of the respondents had good working experience for a period of more than 4 years and thus, the researcher gathered reliable information from knowledgeable and experienced workers or respondents.

4.3 How Best Employee Productivity Can Be Determined and Measured

Table 4.3.7: How employee productivity is determined and measured in M-Nic CRC

Statement on how employee productivity is determined and measured in M-Nic CRC	Freq/%	4	3	2	1	Total
By dividing total sales (output in Ugandan shillings) by total compensation costs (input)	Freq.	160	120	120	0	400
	%	40%	30%	30%	0%	100%
Number of hours worked by an employee regardless of work done	Freq.	0	40	235	125	400
	%	0	10%	59%	31%	100%
Amount of work done by an employee regardless of time limit	Freq.	0	110	220	70	400
	%	0	28%	55%	17%	100%
Amount of an employee's work done within a certain time limit in relation to prior set timeframe	Freq.	180	160	60	0	400
	%	45%	40%	15%	0%	100%
Meeting individual employee's performance targets in line with set organizational objectives	Freq.	125	195	60	20	400
	%	31%	49%	15%	5%	100%
Meeting organizational performance targets in line with overall organization set objectives	Freq.	120	140	50	90	400
	%	30%	35%	12%	23%	100%

Source: Primary Data

As presented in table 4.3.7 above, 40% of the respondents strongly agreed that M-Nic CRC determines and measures employee productivity through dividing total sales by total compensation costs, 30% of the respondents agreed and more than 30% of the respondents disagreed that M-Nic CRC determines and measures employee productivity through dividing total sales by total compensation costs. This implies that M-Nic CRC partly measures its employee's productivity using proportion of total output produced or sales made to total inputs or compensation costs. The interviewed operations (field) manager clarified it with reference to output being for instance, the number of customers served or data collected or data analysed or number of physical items sold like computers. Cross-tabulation using SPSS showed that more females than males strongly agreed and thus female employees value saying thank you to them.

As seen from table 4.3.7 above, 10% of the respondents strongly agreed, 59% disagreed, and 31% strongly disagreed that M-Nic CRC measures its employee productivity through number of hours worked by an employee regardless of work done. In addition to some of the interviewees consenting, by extension it came out clearly that determining employee productivity based on hours worked is not highly applied at M-Nic CRC, like as emphasised by the line manager in-charge of organizational baseline surveys. *"For our research department, hours worked is not an issue but how much work one has produced in a day or week is what matters in terms of measuring research or field employee"* he stated.

As shown from table 4.3.7 above, 28% of the respondents agreed, 55% disagreed, and 17% strongly disagreed that M-Nic CRC measures its employee productivity through the amount of work done by an employee regardless of time limit. It can be seen that most of the respondents disagreed with this measurement and in fact none of the interviewees consented except managers and respondents from the research department where employee productivity was found to be majority based on work done than hours worked like as quoted in the previous paragraph.

The highly supported measure of employee productivity can be further presented as follows (using a pie chart):

Figure 4.3.3: Productivity measurement based on amount of an employee`s work done within a certain time limit in relation to prior set timeframe

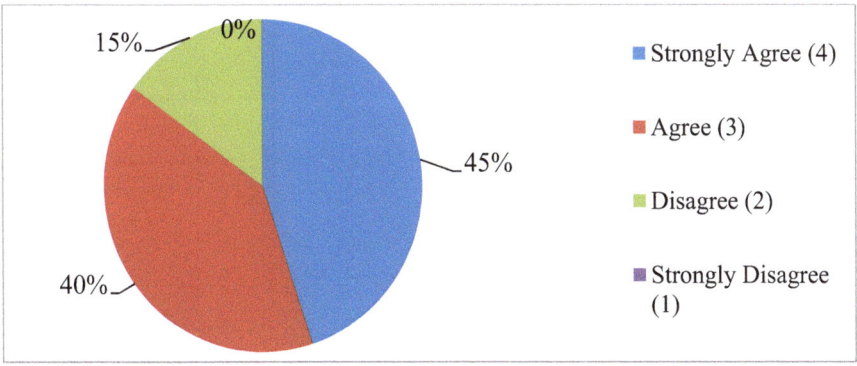

Source: Primary Data

As presented in table 4.3.7 above, 45% of the respondents strongly agreed, 40% agreed, and 15% disagreed that M-Nic CRC measures its employee productivity based on the amount of an employee`s work done within a certain time limit in relation to prior set timeframe. This means that using the amount of work done in a specified period of time is M-Nic CRC`s most preferred determinant basis of employee's productivity. Most of the interviewed researchers and consultants clarified that one's productivity is better measured depending not only on work done but also considering for how long the work has been completed or executed. For instance the senior consultant in the Consultancy department stated, *"customer satisfaction in consultancy can only be achieved if services are delivered on time as stipulated in the contract and thus time is an important benchmark for measuring the department's consulting employees including us the senior consultants"*.

As it is shown from table 4.3.7 above, 31% of the respondents strongly agreed, 49% agreed, 15% disagreed, and 5% strongly disagreed that M-Nic CRC measures its employee productivity based on meeting individual employee's performance targets in line with set organizational objectives and targets. This was less supported as compared to work done in a specified period of time, as equally few interviewees consented. However, all departmental managers admitted that they have individual targets which form part of the firm's general employee productivity measurement basis.

As seen from table 4.3.7 above, 30% of the respondents strongly agreed, 35% agreed, 12% disagreed, and 23% strongly disagreed that M-Nic CRC measures its employee productivity based on meeting organizational performance targets in line with overall organization set objectives. Despite the fact that most of the respondents consenting to this determinant basis, it was also less supported as compared to work done in a specified period of time. Except for one line manager; the human resource officer, all other interviewed managers (consultants and researchers) opposed the measurement based on meeting organizational objectives like one of the field researchers who confirmed that she was not aware of any firm's targets regarding field work except specific assignment and individual targets.

Based on the above presented findings under table 4.3.7 in respect to the objective of finding out how best employee productivity can be determined and measured in business organizations, most of the respondents strongly agreed and agreed that M-Nic CRC measures its employee productivity based on the amount of an employee's work done within a certain time limit in relation to prior set timeframe and target. This means that using the amount of work done in a specified period of time is M-Nic CRC's most preferred determinant basis of employee's productivity. This was followed by measuring employee productivity based on

26

dividing total sales by total compensation costs, as the proportion of total output produced or sales made to total inputs or compensation costs (40% strongly agreed and 30% agreed). This is in line with De-Konink & Griego (2000); Muhammed (2011); and Bloch (2014) who had noted that productivity can be measured based on input and output in different years or based on units of output per labour hour/shift.

Other fairly supported measures of employee productivity as highlighted in table 4.3.7 of the study findings include; meeting individual employee`s performance targets in line with set organizational objectives (31% strongly agreed and 49% agreed), and meeting organizational performance targets in line with overall organization set objectives (30% strongly agreed and 35% agreed). These were earlier also noted by Bennett (2014) and Bloch (2014) as they further emphasised that *"the metric that matters in employee productivity measurement is task completion in terms of individual or organizational set objectives or targets, as against minutes spent at the office"*.

4.4 Various Forms of Simple Employee Recognition Programs used in M-Nic CRC

Table 4.4.8: Various forms of simple employee recognition programs used in M-Nic CRC

Statement on various forms of simple employee recognition programs used in M-Nic CRC	Freq/%	4	3	2	1	Total
Saying thank you	Freq.	180	120	100	0	400
	%	45%	30%	25%	0%	100%
Praises for good work done	Freq.	220	120	60	0	400
	%	55%	30%	15%	0%	100%
Simple gifts	Freq.	140	80	110	70	400
	%	35%	20%	28%	17%	100%
Showing appreciation for employee`s hard-work	Freq.	80	128	132	60	400
	%	20%	32%	33%	15%	100%
Making workplace exceptional	Freq.	72	98	144	86	400
	%	18%	24%	36%	22%	100%
Providing flexible schedule for holidays	Freq.	40	108	72	180	400
	%	10%	27%	18%	45%	100%

Source: Primary Data

As it is seen from table 4.4.8 above, 45% of the respondents had to strongly agree, 30% agreed, and 25% disagreed that saying thank you is ranks among the various forms of simple employee recognition programs embraced by M-Nic CRC. This shows that most of the respondents consented and thus, appreciation of saying thank you by M-Nic CRC managers or supervisors (researchers and consultants) to their subordinates (field or research assistants) as it was further clarified by the interviewed managers. For instance, in his words, the managing director had this to say, *"At M-Nic CRC, we understand our consultancy firm is largely composed of human capital and it is upon this that I have always championed valuing our employees as resourceful assets through big things and simple things which matter like saying thank you".* All employees with experience beyond one year consented, on the same token all highly educated employees (with 1st degree) and employees above 30 years of age equally consented.

The highly mentioned form of simple employee recognition can be further presented graphically as follows (using a bar graph):

Figure 4.4.4: Praises for good work done as an employee recognition form

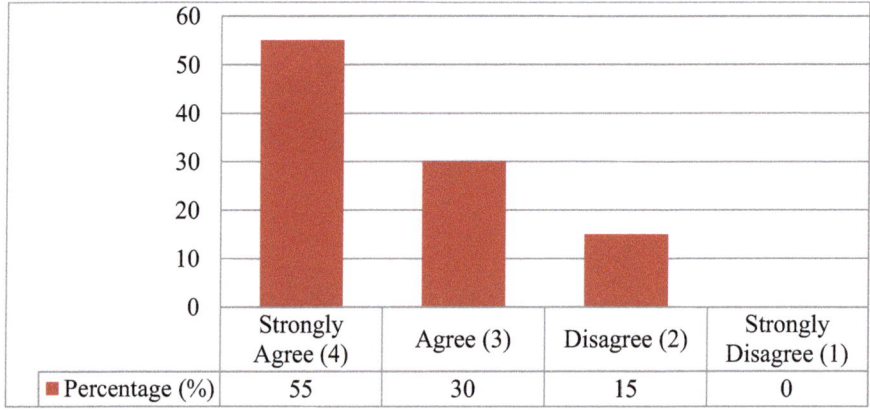

	Strongly Agree (4)	Agree (3)	Disagree (2)	Strongly Disagree (1)
■ Percentage (%)	55	30	15	0

Source: Primary Data

Based on the table 4.4.8 above, 55% of the respondents strongly agreed, 30% agreed, and 15% disagreed that praises for work done take place at M-Nic CRC as among the various forms of simple employee recognition programs. Most of the female employees with less than one year of working experience strongly agreed and therefore praising employees for their work done is highly appreciated at M-Nic CRC. All the interviewees emphasized that

28

they have often shown appreciation for their subordinates' work done especially when in the field collecting client information or when staff have returned from the field for data collection and field surveys.

As presented in table 4.4.8 above, 35% of the respondents strongly agreed, 20% agreed, 28% disagreed, and 17% strongly disagreed that giving simple gifts to employees is recognized at M-Nic CRC. This implies that giving of simple gifts to M-Nic CRC employees is not among the most embraced forms of simple employee recognition programs as a total of 45% respondents opposed it, and as this was contradicting interview findings where most of the interviewees noted that there are a number of simple gifts offered like air time, note books, training, parties, Christmas packages, corporate T-Shirts, corporate caps, pens, protective gears, and many others. One of the Consultants who doubles as the Trainer of Trainees at M-Nic CRC surprisingly voiced loudly, *"Look here Mr., here is the T-Shirt with the firm's logo that I was given as a token from the Marketing Manager as an employee of M-Nic CRC"*

As shown in table 4.4.8 above, 20% of the respondents strongly agreed, 32% agreed, 33% disagreed, and 15% strongly disagreed that showing appreciation for hard-work is being embraced at M-Nic CRC. Many of the questionnaire respondents did not consent with this and this implies that a few of the M-Nic CRC managers or supervisors show appreciation to their employees for their hard-work. However, this was contrary to many of the interviewed researchers and consultants who acknowledged that appreciation was part of M-Nic CRC's embraced forms of employee recognition programs. The human resource manager and the managing director clarified that appreciation is part of the firm with an example of framing and hanging the photo of one of the employee of the year in the office.

As seen from table 4.4.8 above, 18% of the respondents strongly agreed, 24% agreed, 36% disagreed, and 22% strongly disagreed that making workplace as exceptional as possible at M-Nic CRC is among the embraced forms of simple employee recognition programs. This is contrary to interview findings such as the interviewed finance manager who stated that *"we have invested substantial financial resources in beautifying and enhancing our firm's workplace for a better ambience and generally in a bid to make the workplace environment exceptional and friendly for all our employees"*. In line with the study findings, this can be seen that most of the respondents disagreed and thus making work exceptional as among the established ways of enforcing simple employee recognition at M-Nic CRC is not highly appreciated by the firm's overall employees except a few managers.

As presented in the table 4.4.8 above, 10% of the respondents strongly agreed, 27% agreed, 18% disagreed, and 45% of the respondents strongly disagreed that providing flexible schedules for holidays is among the various forms of employee recognition programs found at M-Nic CRC. In line with interviewed managers, this was highly opposed and this means that the holidays given to employees are the normal ones but not as part of employee recognition. Emphasis can be reflected by quoting the words for one of the interviewed departmental managers who lamented, *"the basic common public holidays respected by M-Nic are only those recognised on the Ugandan calendar like labour day, Christmas and Easter holidays, independence day and Uganda martyrs day not others like women's day"*

According to findings as tabulated in table 4.4.8 above in respect of the study objective of identifying various forms of simple employee recognition programs used in business organizations, the majority of the respondents consented that M-Nic CRC appreciates the benefits of praising employees for their good work done (55% strongly agreed and 30% agreed) and equally saying thank you (45% strongly agreed and 30% of them agreed). Findings are actually in line with the words of Harrison (2008) who stated that "There are two aspects to simple employee recognition; identify or realize an opportunity to praise someone and the physical act of doing something to acknowledge and praise people for their good work". Additionally, Heathfield (2004) and Bersin (2012) further noted that there are cheap and free cost employee recognition practices like saying "thank you or well done" which should be embraced by all business organizations.

Like Harter & Killham (2003) who had earlier noted that recognizing people for their good work sends an extremely powerful message to the recipient, the study findings established other less supported forms of employee recognition at M-Nic CRC and these include; showing appreciation to employees especially field researchers and data collectors for their hard work (total of 52% acknowledged), and giving simple gifts to M-Nic CRC employees like air time (Phone recharge card), T-Shirts, caps, note-books, pens and protective gears (total of 55% acknowledged).

4.5 Relationship between simple employee recognition programs and employee productivity

Table 4.5.9: Relationship between simple employee recognition programs and employee productivity in M-Nic CRC

Statement on the relationship between simple employee recognition programs and employee productivity in M-Nic CRC	Freq/%	4	3	2	1	Total
Saying "thank you" to employees by M-Nic CRC managers/supervisors has contributed to achievement of improved employee productivity at M-Nic CRC	Freq.	240	160	0	0	400
	%	60%	40%	0%	0%	100%
Praises for employees' good work done by M-Nic CRC managers/supervisors has contributed to achievement of improved employee productivity at M-Nic CRC	Freq.	248	120	32	0	400
	%	62%	30%	8%	0%	100%
Simple gifts given to employees by M-Nic CRC managers/supervisors has contributed to achievement of improved employee productivity at M-Nic CRC	Freq.	176	108	74	42	400
	%	44%	27%	19%	10%	100%
Showing appreciation for employee's hard-work by M-Nic CRC managers/supervisors has contributed to achievement of improved employee productivity at M-Nic CRC	Freq.	181	107	112	0	400
	%	45%	27%	28%	0%	100%
Making workplace for employees exceptional by M-Nic CRC managers/supervisors has contributed to achievement of improved employee productivity at M-Nic CRC	Freq.	102	147	56	95	400
	%	26%	37%	14%	23%	100%
Provision of flexible schedule for employees' holidays by M-Nic CRC managers/supervisors has contributed to achievement of improved employee productivity at M-Nic CRC	Freq.	31	126	84	159	400
	%	7%	32%	21%	40%	100%

Source: Primary Data

As shown from table 4.5.9 above, 60% of the respondents strongly agreed, and 40% of the respondents agreed that saying "thank you" to employees by M-Nic CRC research and consulting managers has contributed to achievement of improved employee productivity at M-Nic CRC. This implies that actually saying thank contributes much towards improving employee productivity, as it was actually clarified by interviewed research and consulting managers where some of them noted that *"it cost nothing to say thank you"*.

Pearson Correlation between saying thank you and employee productivity

Correlations

		Saying thank you	Employee productivity due to saying thank you
Saying thank you	Pearson Correlation	1.000	.829**
	Sig. (2-tailed)	.	.000
	N	400	400
Employee productivity due to saying thank you	Pearson Correlation	.829**	1.000
	Sig. (2-tailed)	.000	.
	N	400	400

**. Correlation is significant at the 0.01 level (2-tailed).

From the above it can be seen that there is a significant correlation between the two variables, as Pearson correlation between saying thank you and employee productivity is $r = 0.829$. This implies that saying thank you can improve employee`s productivity by 82.9%, and thus a positive significant relationship.

As presented in the table 4.5.9 above, 62% of the respondents strongly agreed, 30% agreed, and 8% disagreed that praises for employees` good work done by M-Nic CRC research and consulting managers/supervisors has contributed to achievement of improved employee productivity at M-Nic CRC. This was also highly recognized by respondents alongside interviewees and thus justifying the relationship between praising for work done and employee`s improved productivity. The point of praising subordinates at M-Nic CRC was greatly substantiated by most of the top and middle level managers as largely revealed by questionnaire findings. For instance, *"I have always made it a point to walk around my department and appreciate every one through praises like good work, well done, you are wonderful employee, and keep it up"* the head of Research department clarified and *"For motivation purposes and to get the best out of the employees, it is very important to praise them like as it is a large part of our tradition here at M-Nic CRC"* the head of Consultancy department further justified.

Pearson Correlation between praises for good work done and employee productivity

Correlations

		Praises for work done	Employee productivity due to praises for work done
Praises for work done	Pearson Correlation	1.000	.882**
	Sig. (2-tailed)	.	.000
	N	400	400
Employee productivity due to praises for work done	Pearson Correlation	.882**	1.000
	Sig. (2-tailed)	.000	.
	N	400	400

**. Correlation is significant at the 0.01 level (2-tailed).

As it can be seen from above Pearson correlation of $r = 0.888$, this shows that there is a positive significant relationship between praising an employee for his good work done and that of employee productivity. Thus, improved employee productivity can be attributed to praises for good work done by 88.8%, as aptly justified by the above Pearson Correlation.

As shown in the table 4.5.9 above, 44% of the respondents strongly agreed, 27% agreed, 19% disagreed, and 10% strongly disagreed that simple gifts given to employees` by M-Nic CRC research and consulting managers or supervisors has contributed to achievement of improved employee productivity at M-Nic CRC. Most of the respondents to the questionnaires and interviewees consented but less as compared to saying thank you and praises, and thus, a slight relationship between simple gifts and employee productivity.

Pearson Correlation between offered simple gifts and employee productivity

Correlations

		Offer of simple gifts	Employee productivity due to offered simple gifts
Offer of simple gifts	Pearson Correlation	1.000	.909**
	Sig. (2-tailed)	.	.000
	N	400	400
Employee productivity due to offered simple gifts	Pearson Correlation	.909**	1.000
	Sig. (2-tailed)	.000	.
	N	400	400

**. Correlation is significant at the 0.01 level (2-tailed).

The Pearson Correlation of *r = 0.909* shows that there is a significant relationship between simple gifts and employee productivity. This means that there would be great improved employee productivity at M-Nic CRC to the tune of 90.9% if the company was offering simple gifts in form of employee recognition (since most of the respondents explained that the offered simple gifts are normal and not-recognition oriented gifts).

As seen from table 4.5.9 above, 45% of the respondents strongly agreed, 27% of them agreed, and 28% of respondents disagreed that showing appreciation for employee's hard-work by M-Nic CRC research and consulting managers or supervisors has contributed to achievement of improved employee productivity at M-Nic CRC. The bigger percentage of respondents and all the interviewed managers strongly agreed that appreciating employee for their efforts has catalysed the growth and success of the firm due to improved employee productivity and organizational performance. This was evidenced further with statements like *"I can say that a combination of praising and appreciating employees has seen the firm grow day by day"* from the firm's managing director. This implies that there is a significant relationship between praising or appreciation and employee productivity.

Pearson Correlation between appreciation for hard-work and employee productivity

Correlations

		Appreciation for hard-work	Employee productivity due to hardwork appreciation
Appreciation for hard-work	Pearson Correlation	1.000	.864**
	Sig. (2-tailed)	.	.000
	N	400	400
Employee productivity due to hardwork appreciation	Pearson Correlation	.864**	1.000
	Sig. (2-tailed)	.000	.
	N	400	400

**. Correlation is significant at the 0.01 level (2-tailed).

As shown from the above Pearson Correlation of *r = 0.864* and as per the findings under table 4.4.9, this means that if M-Nic CRC research and consulting management or supervisors keep appreciating for their subordinates' hard-work, then there would be improved employee productivity by 86.4% as the justification of the relationship between appreciation for one's hard-work and one's productivity.

As it is seen from table 4.5.9 above, 26% of the respondents strongly agreed, 37% agreed, 14% disagreed, and 23% strongly disagreed that making workplace for employees exceptional by M-Nic CRC research and consulting managers or supervisors has contributed to achievement of improved employee productivity at M-Nic CRC. Many of the respondents and a few of the interviewees opposed positive contribution to productivity from making work exceptional, and thus, a slight relationship with few of the respondents consenting. Contrary views equally came from interviewed managers like one of the line managers who emotionally stated that *"despite the firm's efforts of renovating the premises with attracting paintings and clean workplace, this has not greatly moved me since I mind about how much do I take home as salary"*

Pearson Correlation between exceptional workplace and employee productivity

Correlations

		Making workplace exceptional	Employee productivity due to exceptional worplace
Making workplace exceptional	Pearson Correlation	1.000	.900**
	Sig. (2-tailed)	.	.000
	N	400	400
Employee productivity due to exceptional worplace	Pearson Correlation	.900**	1.000
	Sig. (2-tailed)	.000	.
	N	400	400

**. Correlation is significant at the 0.01 level (2-tailed).

The above Pearson Correlation of $r = 0.90$ shows that the workplace at M-Nic CRC had it been exceptional, employee productivity would been improved by 90%. Due to the fact that most of the respondents under table 4.4.9 had disagreed that the workplace at M-Nic CRC is exceptional, the Pearson Correlation (r) of 0.9 justifies how lack of exceptional work negatively affects employee productivity by 90%.

As shown from table 4.5.9 above, 7% of the respondents strongly agreed, 32% agreed, 21% disagreed, and 40% strongly disagreed that provision of flexible schedule for employees` holidays by M-Nic CRC research and consulting managers or supervisors has contributed to achievement of improved employee productivity at M-Nic CRC. Due to absence of flexible schedules aimed at employee recognition as prior noted under table 4.4.9 (inclusive of interview findings), it was clearly shown above that there is no relationship as most of the respondents strongly disagreed that provision of flexible schedule for employees` holidays by M-Nic CRC managers/supervisors has contributed to achievement of improved employee productivity at M-Nic CRC.

Pearson Correlation between flexible holiday schedules and employee productivity

Correlations

		Providing flexible holiday schedules	Employee productivity due to flexible holidays
Providing flexible holiday schedules	Pearson Correlation	1.000	.957**
	Sig. (2-tailed)	.	.000
	N	400	400
Employee productivity due to flexible holidays	Pearson Correlation	.957**	1.000
	Sig. (2-tailed)	.000	.
	N	400	400

**. Correlation is significant at the 0.01 level (2-tailed).

With the Pearson Correlation of *r = 0.957*, this implies that provision of flexible holiday schedules to employees improves their productivity by 95.7%. With particular reference to questionnaire findings under table 4.4.9 where most of the respondents disagreed that providing flexible schedules for holidays is among the various forms of employee recognition programs found at M-Nic CRC, this further justifies how absence of flexible holiday schedules greatly affects employee productivity.

As per the study findings presented under Table 4.5.9 regarding the study objective of examining the relationship between simple employee recognition and employee productivity, many of the simple employee recognition programs contribute towards achievement of improved employee productivity especially just saying thank you to employee or any subordinate like research assistants, justified by Pearson Correlation of r = 0.829. 100% of the respondents (60% strongly agreed and 40% agreed) acknowledged the relationship between saying thank you and improved employee productivity like as it was earlier noted by Harrison (2008).

It was further established that there is significant relationship between praising employees for their work done and employee productivity (62% strongly agreed and 30% agreed); significant relationship between showing appreciation for employee`s hard work and employee productivity (45% strongly agreed and 27% agreed) and justified by Pearson

Correlation of r = 0.882; insignificant relationship between giving simple gifts to employees or subordinates and employee productivity (44% strongly agreed and 27% agreed); and also insignificant relationship between making work exceptional for workers and employee productivity (26% strongly agreed and 37% agreed). In line with Chaire, et al., (2010) who had noted that satisfaction and productivity rises when employees` work is valued and Luciano (2012) further clarified that recognition programs help any organization to achieve improved employee productivity.

4.6 Strategies of how to improve employee productivity through simple employee recognition programs

Table 4.6.10: Strategies of how to improve employee productivity through simple employee recognition programs

Statement on the strategies of how to improve employee productivity through simple employee recognition programs in M-Nic CRC	Freq/%	4	3	2	1	Total
Deciding with employees what is to be achieved through employee recognition efforts	Freq.	94	156	118	32	400
	%	23%	39%	30%	8%	100%
Creation of goals and action plans for employee recognition programs	Freq.	208	192	0	0	400
	%	52%	48%	0%	0%	100%
Ensuring fairness, clarity and consistency as they are important in employee recognition	Freq.	223	97	37	43	400
	%	56%	25%	9%	11%	100%
Employee recognition approaches and content must also be inconsistent	Freq.	85	148	80	87	400
	%	21%	37%	20%	22%	100%
Being as special as it can be, in telling the individual exactly why he/she is receiving the recognition	Freq.	44	124	207	25	400
	%	11%	31%	52%	6%	100%
Offering employee recognition as close to the recognizing event as possible	Freq.	168	104	112	16	400
	%	42%	26%	28%	4%	100%

Source: Primary Data

According to the data shown in table 4.6.10 above, 23% of the respondents strongly agreed, 39% respondents agreed, 30% respondents disagreed, and 8% of them strongly disagreed that M-Nic CRC decides with employees what is to be achieved through employee recognition efforts. Most of the ordinary employees are the respondents who answered (ticked) disagree and strongly disagree. This can be seen that to a lesser extent, employees especially research field workers (assistant employees, data collectors and analysts) are involved in decision making regarding employee recognition programs and this response was also supported by interview findings as some managers acknowledged that *"it is good to involve employees in decision making"* even though some of the heads of departments further emphasized that *"ordinary employees should not be included in all decisions like strategic planning decisions"*.

The highly recommended strategy by the respondents for improving employee productivity through simple employee recognition can be further presented using a doughnut pie chart:

Figure 4.6.5: Creation of goals/plans for employee recognition programs as a strategy for improve employee productivity through simple employee recognition programs

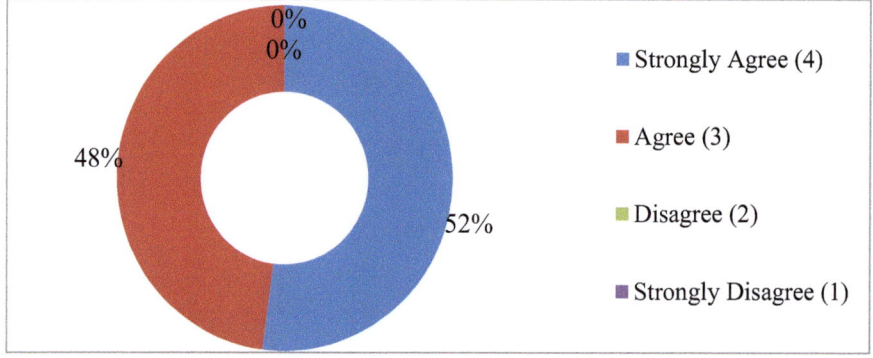

Source: Primary Data

As explicitly highlighted in the table 4.6.10 above, 52% of the respondents strongly agreed, and 48% agreed that there is creation of goals and action plans for employee recognition programs at M-Nic CRC. The interviewed human resource manager in addition to all interviewed managers noted that the firm`s goals are always communicated at the start of every year to all employees of the firm. Like as it was justified by the interviewed research and consulting managers, this implies that most of the M-Nic CRC management and employees are satisfied with the company`s goals and action plans towards employee`s recognition.

As presented in the table 4.6.10 above, 56% of the respondents strongly agreed, 25% agreed, 9% disagreed, and 11% strongly disagreed that there is ensuring of fairness, clarity and consistency while recognizing employees of M-Nic CRC. Most of the respondents strongly agreed and this means that the few available simple employee recognition programs are equitably offered to all employees. All the research and consulting interviewees clarified that there is no any form of discrimination at M-Nic CRC and thus equality and fairness, like the words of human resource manager who categorically stated *"the firm subscribes to anti-discrimination policies and we cherish diversity as depicted from our policy manuals and data base"*. This was substantiated by the researcher where employees` register (documents and database) showed different ethnicity in terms of religions like Muslims, Protestants, and Catholics plus different tribes such as Acholi, Banyankole, Batooro, Japhadhola, and Baganda.

As seen from table 4.6.10 above, 21% of the respondents strongly agreed, 37% agreed, 20% disagreed, and 22% strongly disagreed that employee recognition approaches and content must also be inconsistent. This was fairly supported and this means that inconsistency in simple employee recognition programs are not highly appreciated by management and employees of M-Nic CRC. A few of the research and consulting interviewed managers supported inconsistency and others declined from recommending for inconsistencies while offering simple employee recognition programs.

As shown from table 4.6.10 above, 11% of the respondents strongly agreed, 31% agreed, 52% disagreed, and 6% strongly disagreed that M-Nic CRC should make it special as it can be in telling the individual exactly why he/she is receiving the recognition. In line with interviewed research and consulting managers, this was highly opposed and this means that it is not necessary to make it special as most of the M-Nic CRC management and employees disagreed. *"Employee recognition should be in form of surprises but not publically known as special if it is to achieve its intended purpose like employee motivation"* the marketing manager contrary stated.

As it can be seen from table 4.6.10 above, 42% of the respondents strongly agreed, 26% agreed, 28% disagreed, and 4% strongly disagreed with the strategy of offering employee recognition as close to the recognizing event as possible. Most of the respondents strongly agreed and this implies that good timing for when to offer simple employee recognition is crucial to the satisfaction of receiving employee. All the managers who were interviewed credited themselves on planning and proper timing regarding effecting/implementing company's activities including employee recognition programs. Most of the interviewed managers attributed success of M-Nic CRC (*being among the leading research and consulting firms in Uganda*) to their effective management.

All the respondents under table 4.6.10 as per the presented findings above in respect of the study objective of establishing strategies of how to improve employee productivity through simple employee recognition programs, they acknowledged that M-Nic CRC creates goals and action plans for employee recognition programs and this has contributed to achievement of improved employee productivity (52% of the respondents strongly agreed and 48% agreed). This conforms to the views of World at Work (2011) through Irvine (2012) who reported that employee involvement in action plans motivate employees and contributes to improvement of employee productivity. However, some of the respondents denied being involved in deciding what simple employee recognition programs that M-Nic CRC embraces and this is contrary to the plea made by Heathfield (2004) that appreciating participation while deciding what is to be achieved through employee recognition efforts is crucial for any organization.

M-Nic CRC was further credited to a bigger extent by most of the respondents that it ensures fairness, clarity and consistency while recognizing employees, and thus contributing to achievement of improved productivity due to the fact that the few available simple employee recognition programs are equitably offered to all employees (56% strongly agreed). This is in agreement with McGrory-Dixon (2013) who had earlier observed that it is important to recognize all people who contributed to a success equally. Heathfield (2004) and McGrory-Dixon (2013) further recommended for the strategy of offering employee recognition as close to the recognizing event as possible, which is in line with the study findings, as most of the respondents (42%) strongly agreed and this implies that good timing for when to offer simple employee recognition is crucial to the satisfaction of receiving employee for improved employee productivity.

Generally, respondents characteristics greatly affect their attitude and influence the extent to which firm's simple employee recognition programs affect their productivity. For instance, the more the working experience, the more preference of simple non-financial employee recognition to financial recognition programs and the more the educational level for the employee the lesser preference of non-financial simple employee recognition programs to physical and financial employee recognition programs.

This was clearly analysed using cross tabulations with examples shown below;

Gender of Respondents * Saying thank you Crosstabulation

			Saying thank you			
			Disagree	Agree	Strongly agree	Total
Gender of Respondents	Male	Count	60	46	49	155
		% within Saying thank you	60.0%	38.3%	27.2%	38.8%
	Female	Count	40	74	131	245
		% within Saying thank you	40.0%	61.7%	72.8%	61.3%
Total		Count	100	120	180	400
		% within Saying thank you	100.0%	100.0%	100.0%	100.0%

Based on cross-tabulation, most of the female employees consented (73% strongly agreed) that simple employee recognition have a positive effect on their motivation and productivity like saying thank you and appreciation.

Age group of Respondents * Saying thank you Crosstabulation

			Saying thank you			
			Disagree	Agree	Strongly agree	Total
Age group of Respondents	20-30 years	Count	17	54	99	170
		% within Saying thank you	17.0%	45.0%	55.0%	42.5%
	31-40 years	Count	56	33	81	170
		% within Saying thank you	56.0%	27.5%	45.0%	42.5%
	above 40 years	Count	27	33		60
		% within Saying thank you	27.0%	27.5%		15.0%
Total		Count	100	120	180	400
		% within Saying thank you	100.0%	100.0%	100.0%	100.0%

It was further found that middle-aged or old people are not moved by (do not treasure) simple employee recognition programs like gifts, saying thank you and flexible holidays unlike younger employees aged 20 to 30 years (55% strongly agreed).

Category of Respondents * Offer of simple gifts Crosstabulation

			Offer of simple gifts				Total
			Strongly disagree	Disagree	Agree	Strongly agree	
Category of Respondents	Ordinary employees	Count		66	70	134	270
		% within Offer of simple gifts		60.0%	87.5%	95.7%	67.5%
	Lower management	Count	61	25	2	2	90
		% within Offer of simple gifts	87.1%	22.7%	2.5%	1.4%	22.5%
	Middle management	Count	8	17	6	1	32
		% within Offer of simple gifts	11.4%	15.5%	7.5%	.7%	8.0%
	Top management	Count	1	2	2	3	8
		% within Offer of simple gifts	1.4%	1.8%	2.5%	2.1%	2.0%
Total		Count	70	110	80	140	400
		% within Offer of simple gifts	100.0%	100.0%	100.0%	100.0%	100.0%

As depicted above, under the cross-tabulation of levels of management and offering of simple gifts, most of the ordinary employees as compared to managers concurred (96% strongly agreed) that simple employee recognition like offer of gifts greatly contribute to their productivity.

CHAPTER FIVE: SUMMARIES, CONCLUSIONS, RECOMMENDATIONS, FURTHER RESEARCH AREAS, AND REFLECTIONS

5.1 Introduction

This chapter is primarily focused on the summaries of major findings both from the literature and primary research, conclusions, specific recommendations, areas for further research, and self-reflections. The focus of this chapter was based on the relationship between simple employee recognition and employee productivity in business organizations in Uganda, a case study of M-Nic CRC Ltd.

Further to that, conclusions and recommendations were made based mainly on the findings prior presented in line with the study objectives; thereby finding out how best employee productivity can be determined and measured in business organizations, also identified various forms of simple employee recognition programs used in business organizations, examining the relationship between simple employee recognition and employee productivity, and establishing strategies of how best to improve employee productivity through simple employee recognition programs.

5.2 Summary of Key Findings from the Literature

5.2.1 How employee productivity is determined and measured in Business Organizations

The emphasised basic determinant measure of employee productivity as stated in the related literature reviewed was output per worker hour (units of output per labour hour or shift like as emphasised by Laura 2010; Muhammed 2011; and Corbett et al., 2012). Other noted measures of employee productivity in business organizations included; task completion time in terms of individual and organizational set objectives or targets as noted by Bennett (2014) and Bloch (2014), nature of the work done (Glascock, 2013), and sales made or customers brought on board (Corbett et al., 2012).

5.2.2 Various Forms of Simple Employee Recognition Programs used in Business Organizations

Saying thank you was the most noted outstanding form of simple employee recognition as discussed by the different authors of the literature review for instance, Balle (2013); Bolton

(2013); and Frost (2014), all of them concurred that *"no matter how large or small the company is, and likewise, no matter how large or small the token of appreciation is, thanking someone for their patronage or hard work is just as good a catalyst for peak employee productivity or performance at a cheap cost as any other employee motivation programs"*. Other well documented low or no cost simple employee recognition programs included but not limited to the following; appreciation for employees` hard work (Brandenberg, 2013 and Glascock, 2013), having a picture of the employee of the month (for instance) receiving his or her award and/or posing with their superiors and send it home via courier or framing an employee of the month or year (as the case may be) and place it at the reception or entrance area (Bonser, et al., 2013), giving extra day of paid time off (Laura, 2010), special parking space for high performing employee of the month (Martin, 2014), recognizing employee of the month with banquet of flowers or a framed poster or card (Laura, 2010 & Martin, 2014), morning coffees, gifts, and lunch (Brandenberg, 2013).

5.2.3 Relationship between simple employee recognition programs and employee productivity in Business Organizations

There were contradicting views regarding the nature and the extent to which simple employee recognition programs go a very long way to positively affect employees` productivity and performance within a set time period. For instance, Irvine (2012) lamented that employee recognition often goes with associated costly expenses and that end the author cautioned that employee reward decision can be of great danger to stressed organizations. It could weigh heavily on the organization' operating cost he further alluded. Contrary to those views, authors like Chaire, et al., (2010) noted that measuring employee performance is a key strategy for organizational success as a result of employee recognition and improved productivity, in addition to Cavanaugh (2014) who emphasised that employee recognition creates a better working environment that would enable employees improve their productivity by enhancing their performance.

Therefore, most of the authors (like Heathfield, 2004; Slusher, 2010; Balle, 2013; and Frost, 2014) as highlighted in the reviewed related literature observed among other things that there is a relationship between simple employee recognition and improved employee productivity and performance, if appropriate forms of simple employee recognition programs are effectively implemented.

44

5.2.4 Strategies of how to improve employee productivity through simple employee recognition programs in Business Organizations

Recognizing and rewarding employees was the most talked about strategy in which a larger percentage of authors suggested as stated in the reviewed related literature and among the high profile authors who added their voices include Harter & Killham (2003), Andy (2010), and Brandenberg (2013). Among other highlighted strategies for improved employee productivity and high performance through simple employee recognition programs include; offering holiday meals, respecting holiday days like Independence and Christmas days (Frost & Martin, 2014), organizing thanks giving services, allowing longer lunch and dinner breaks for employees, through appreciation messages and praising of employees (Laura, 2010 and Martin, 2014), and offering formal and informal monetary or non-monetary recognition rewards to peak performing employees (Luciano, 2012).

5.3 Summary of Key Findings from the Primary Research

5.3.1 How employee productivity is determined and measured in M-Nic CRC

Most of the respondents interviewed strongly agreed (45%) and 40% of them agreed that M-Nic CRC should measure its employee productivity based on the amount of an employee's work done within a certain time limit in relation to prior set timeframe and targets (Table 4.3.7 of the study findings in chapter four). Others fairly supported the measures of employee productivity which includes; meeting individual employees (a total of 80% of the respondents consented – both strongly agreed and agreed) or organizational performance targets in line with set organizational objectives (65% for both respondents who strongly agreed and agreed as per Table 4.3.7).

5.3.2 Various Forms of Simple Employee Recognition Programs used in M-Nic CRC

The majority of the respondents consented that M-Nic CRC should actually appreciate the benefits of praising employees whenever they perform remarkably well and/or meet their targets (55% of the respondents strongly agreed whilst 30% of them agreed) and sizeable number equally agreed that saying thank you actually motivates them (45% and 30% of the respondents strongly agreed and agreed respectively, as per Table 4.4.8 of the study findings). Other less supported forms of employee recognition presented under Table 4.4.8 and discussed thereafter in chapter four include; showing appreciation to employees for their hard-work, and giving simple gifts.

5.3.3 Relationship between simple employee recognition programs and employee productivity in M-Nic CRC

Many of the simple employee recognition programs contribute positively towards achievement of improved employee productivity and performance especially just saying thank you to employee or any subordinate, with r = 0.829 (83%) as presented and discussed in chapter four of the study findings (Table 4.5.9). This is in line with existing literature like as earlier noted by various authors such as Balle (2013); Bolton (2013); and Frost (2014). It was further established under the 3rd study objective (4.5 of the study findings) that there is positive significant relationship between praising employees for their work done on the one hand and employee productivity on the other hand (with r = 882); and equally positive significant relationship between showing appreciation for employee's hard-work on the one hand and employee productivity (with r = 0.864) on the other hand.

5.3.4 Strategies of how to improve employee productivity through simple employee recognition programs at M-Nic CRC

All the respondents (100% of them) as indicated in Table 4.6.10 of the study findings acknowledged (52% of them strongly agreed whilst 48% of them agreed) that M-Nic CRC should in essence create goals and action plans for employee recognition programs and they went further to allude to the fact that such actions have positively contributed to the achievement of improved employee productivity and enhanced performance as a result of high motivation. However, some of the respondents denied being involved in deciding making regarding simple employee recognition programs (total of 38% strongly disagreed and disagreed under the same Table 4.6.10 as per the first statement/dimension). M-Nic CRC was further credited for ensuring fairness, clarity and consistency while recognizing employees at the right time and with the requisite reward (81% consented, that is, both strongly agreed and agreed), and thus contributing to achievement of improved productivity.

5.4 Conclusion

Based on the presented, discussed and summarised findings of the study whose primary purpose was to critically analyse the relationship between simple employee recognition and that of employee productivity in business organizations, and in line with the study's specific objectives, the study's combined main conclusions are as stated hereunder;

☞ There are a number of forms for simple employee recognition with appreciation and praising employees being the outstanding preferred recognition programs as indicated by majority of the respondents.

☞ Simple employee recognition programs contribute as much towards achieving improved employee productivity and as towards organizational performance due to improved productivity.

☞ There is a significant positive relationship between simple employee recognition and that of employee productivity and high performance.

☞ Embracement of strategic cheap and simple recognition programs like saying thank you, praises for good work done and appreciation for employee`s hard-work, enhances employee productivity and motivates them to do wonders on the job.

5.5 Recommendations

5.5.1 Provision of Good Ambiance and generally friendly Working Conditions.

Providing a friendly working environment for workers is less expensive and is highly likely to get the most value out of the employees. Working in a poor working environment has the tendency to sab enthusiasm and motivation out of employees with a corresponding low productivity as a result of poor performance. Working in an environment indoors under artificial lights for 8+ hours a day or noisy place or dirty place can be draining, and well, downright depressing. M-Nic CRC`s offices should be expanded enough to provide its staff with ample space and comfort (not only for work but also for breaks and social gatherings), alongside good ambiance. Additionally, M-Nic CRC, as well as other organizations and all employees should always maintain a hygienic office, keep things tidy and organized, and provide a spacious and quiet room where people can work in a peaceful environment away from the general office distractions.

5.5.2 Respecting Breaks and Offering Special Holiday Days.

M-Nic CRC should not only embrace normal holidays (as noted by research findings) but also offer special holidays like "M-Nic CRC Day". Most employees get satisfied with their jobs due to a number of less costly factors including the desire of having a break during working hours and after expected working hours for various reasons. Some employees rest or enjoy work breaks or off duty periods through the indulgence in personal activities or having a complete rest at home. Denial of breaks such as lunch break and after expected official working hour break or holidays like national independence holiday and Christ-mass holidays will demoralise such workers and consequently affect their performances; it has a corresponding low moral that ultimately affect their performance. It therefore goes without saying there is the absolutely need for employers not to over work their employees without respecting breaks be they for launch, public holidays or for welfare reasons.

5.5.3 The Need for improved and Strong Supervisor - Employee Relationship.

The way supervisors and managers relate to their sub-ordinates matters a lot and it can greatly affect employee performance. Gone are the days where supervisors treated their subordinates in a subdued manner in such a way that they don't even feel free to ask them for anything which has the tendency to undermine mutual working relationship. Despite financial and other non-financial rewards and incentives, an employee like a Research Assistant at M-Nic CRC will never have peace at work or tolerate a bad manager or supervisor (Senior Researcher or Research Field Supervisor). This means that a good relationship between the manager or supervisor would motivate employee to work harder and remain loyal to the employing company. There is therefore the absolute need for a much more camaraderie type of relationship between managers or supervisors and their staff.

5.5.4 Keeping Promises, Provision of Timely Feedback and Respecting Employees.

It takes no coin to fulfil promises made to employees through effective communication (timely feedbacks) and through respecting employee needs or expectations. Not keeping promises and not communicating in a timely manner why the honour promises has the ability to vastly erode mutual trust and respect in the work place. All business organizations like M-Nic CRC are reminded that *"keeping promises, effective communication and respect can be simple and less costly things but powerful motivators, just as its unpleasant twins, failed promises, lack of respect, and poor communication have the opposite effects"*. When employees feel genuinely respected (always assuming it's warranted), they are much more likely "to go the extra mile" to help a company succeed. There is therefore no gainsaying that mutual respect, not breaking promises and a timely and direct line of communication in the work place will no doubt raise staff moral and by extension the desire to perform highly.

5.6 Areas for Further Studies

Possible future areas that the researcher on any other might wish to look into for further studies or research are listed but not limited to the following:

i.   The impact of costly financial rewards on the financial performance of business organizations in Tanzania

ii.   The contribution of manager - employee relationship towards employee commitment at work in business organizations in Uganda

iii. The impact of non-financial rewards and incentives on the organizational financial performance in Kenya

iv.   The effects of non-traditional security problems like Ebola Virus Disease on the performance of businesses organizations in the Mano River Union Countries (Sierra Leone, Liberia and Guinea)

5.7 Knowledge and skills

The researcher's knowledge and skills have already been depicted in line with the prior delineated chapters of; introduction to the study, critically reviewed literature, expounded methodology, presentation of study findings alongside analysis and interpretation of findings, and discussion of findings alongside conclusions and recommendations.

Generally, appropriate practical knowledge and skills have been acquired by the researcher in due course of the study. In addition to theoretical knowledge gained during the academic study sessions, general and specific practical knowledge and skills have been acquired more specifically regarding;

☞ Knowledge on how to measure and determine employee productivity, knowledge on various forms of simple employee recognition programs, knowledge on the relationship between simple employee recognition and employee productivity, and knowledge on the best strategies to improve employee recognition towards improving employee productivity.

☞ Documentation skills, report writing skills, communication skills, presentation skill, computer skills, information-based problem-solving skills, and analytical skill. There is no way the researcher could have done all this report without improving his skills. It was indeed an eye opener.

☞ There is sometimes difference between how offices in the main cities operate as against those in the small towns. The research learnt to appreciate the challenges faced by workers further away from the major cities such as unreliable internet connectivity and poor transportation facilities. If the researcher is faced by such issues in real life as a staff he would now be able to cope with such situations.

REFERENCES

Andy, J.S. & Slusher, J., 2010. *Importance of Measuring and Managing Employee Performance: How to Maximise Employee Productivity*. Retrieved from: http://www.ehow.com/employee-performance-and-productivity.html

Atambo, W. N. et al. 2013. *The Role of Employee Incentives on Performance: A Survey of Public Hospitals in Kenya. Global Business and Economics Research Journal*, 2(12): 29-44. http://www.globejournal.org

Aviva, S., (2011). *Why Invest in Staff Recognition Schemes.* http://www.thevouchershop.co.uk/staff-recognition/

Bennett, H., 2014. *Simple Ways to Improve Employee Utilization and Productivity: HR Comp on Measuring Employee Productivity.* http://www.hrcom.com/productivity

Bersin, J., 2012. *New Research Unlock the Secret of Employees Recognition.* Retrieved from http://www.forbes.com/employee-recognition

Bloch, D., 2014. *Simple Ways to Track and Measure Employee Productivity.* Retrieved in September 2014 from AllBusiness.com

Bolton, D., 2013. *The Importance and Benefits of Employee Rewards and Recognition.* Yahoo Contributor Network.

Bonser, C. Balle, L. Brandenberg, D., 2013. *Simple Employee Recognition Incentives and Rewards: How to Keep Recognition Awards Simple.* Retrieved from http://www.ehow.com/simple-employee-recognition.html and

Caon, V., 2012. *Siemens UK Wins Award For Employee Recognition.* www.employeebenefits.co.uk/...uk...employee-recognition/15210.article

Chaire, et al., 2010. *Theoretical Approaches and a Profile of Employee Recognition.* Canada. Can be accessed from http://www.cgsst.com/eng/expression/employee-recognition

Corbett, E. Gordon, C., Marcia, R.S., 2012. *Measuring Employee Productivity.* Toolkit Staff. Retrieved on Retrieved on 16th September, 2014 from http://www.bizfilings.com/toolkit

De-Konink, T. & Griego, O. V., 2000. *Predictors of Learning Organizations: A Human Resource Development Practitioner's Perspective.* The Learning Organization: An International Journal, 7(1), 5-12.

Frost, S., Cavanaugh, B. & Martin, R., 2014. *Simple Employee Recognition: Ways of Recognising Employee for Improved Productivity.* Ehow Contributions. Retrieved from http://www.ehow.com/list/7627591-5145164-6050328-thank-you-employee-recognition

Glascock, J., (2013). *Employee Appreciation is Equal to Employee Productivity.* Retrieved in November 2013, http://www.sodexomotive.com/incentives

Harrison, K., 2008. *Creative Ideas For Employee Recognition: Why Employee Recognition Is So Important.* Retrieved from www.cuttingedgepr.com, Australia, Cutting Edge PR.

Harter, J.K., Schmidt, F.L., & Killham, E.A., 2003. *Employee Engagement, Satisfaction, and Business-Unit-Level Outcomes: A Meta-Analysis.* Washington DC: The Gallup Organization, Gallup Press.

Heathfield, S., 2004. *Employee Recognition and Employee Engagement.* Gallup Inc., research via About.com Human Resources. www.about.com

Irvine, D., 2012. *Culture & Recognition Matters to Workers everywhere in the World: NEW Winning with a Culture of Recognition.* In World at Work (2011), Recognition Strategies http://www.chinadaily.com.cn/cndy/2012-01/10/content_14410584.htm and www.recognizethisblog.com/.../manage-costs-of-employee-recognition-i...

Laura, W., 2010. *How Can We Best Measure Worker Productivity.* The Journal of Occupational and Environmental Medicine. Publication of the American College of Occupational and Environmental Medicine (ACOEM). Retrieved in September, 2014 from ehstoday.com

Luciano, A., 2012. *Employee Recognition. Company Has Recognition Programs Employees.* Retrieved from http://info.tharperobbins.com/blog/Recognition-Programs

Muhammed, A., 2011. *Productivity Measurement. University of Punjab,* http://www.pu.edu.pk/faculty/descriptions.asp?faculty=66004

52

Ntabgoba, J., 2013. *MTN Uganda Recognises Employees Performance and Excellence.* www.mtn.co.ug/.../mtn-Uganda-recognises-Employee.aspx

Odiya, J. N., 2009. *Scholarly Writing: Research Proposals and Reports in APA or MLA Publication Style.* 1st Edition, Kampala, Makerere University Printery.

Sekaran, U., 2003. *Research Methods or Business Skills Building Approach.* John Wiley, New York.

APPENDICES

Appendix i: Questionnaire for Respondents

Introduction

Dear respondent, my name is Bockarie Sama Banya a student from University of Wales and am pursuing a Masters Degree in Business Administration. I would like you to spare some time and answer the following questions. The responses you provide will be treated with utmost confidentiality and used for academic purposes only.

(Please tick/answer the appropriate alternative).

SECTION A: BIO DATA

1. Sex:

a) Female ☐   b) Male ☐

2. Age of Respondents (years)

a) Below 20 ☐   b) 20 – 30 ☐

c) 31 – 40 ☐   d) Above 41 ☐

3. Level of Education

a) Secondary & below ☐   b) Certificate/Diploma ☐

c) Bachelors degree ☐   d) Masters & beyond ☐

4. Category of respondent

a) Top management ☐   b) Middle management ☐

c) Lower management ☐   d) Ordinary worker ☐

5. For how long have you been working with M-Nic CRC?

a) Less than a year ☐   b) 1 - 5 years ☐   c) 6 years & above ☐

SECTION B: OBJECTIVES

How best employee productivity can be determined and measured in business organizations

Please indicate by whether you strongly agree (4), or agree (3), or disagree (2), strongly disagree (1), in the statements where applicable.

6. The following are the best ways how employee productivity is determined and measured in M-Nic CRC;	1	2	3	4
Basing on the number of hours spent doing work				
The amount of work done by an employee				
Resources utilized in doing the work				
Basing on the work done in consideration of time spent				
Based on the targets or objectives met or achieved				
Number of customers worked on or served by an employee				
Others (specify)				

Various forms of simple employee recognition programs used in M-Nic CRC

Please indicate by whether you strongly agree (4), or agree (3), or disagree (2), strongly disagree (1), in the statements where applicable.

7. The following are the various forms of simple employee recognition programs used in M-Nic CRC;	1	2	3	4
Saying Thank You!				
Praises for good work done				
Simple gifts				
Showing appreciation for employee`s hard-work				
Making workplace exceptional				
Providing flexible schedule for holidays				
Others (specify)				

Relationship between simple employee recognition and employee productivity in M-Nic CRC

Please indicate by whether you strongly agree (4), or agree (3), or disagree (2), strongly disagree (1), in the statements where applicable.

8. The following are the statements depicting the a relationship between simple employee recognition and employee productivity in M-Nic CRC;	1	2	3	4
Simple employee recognition programs increase job satisfaction and thus improved employee productivity				
Employees respond to appreciation expressed in recognition of their good work and thus increased satisfaction and productivity				
Simple employee recognition programs motivates employees to work-hard and thus improving their productivity				
Simple employee recognition programs build positive and productive workplace, which results into improved productivity				
Unfriendly & wrongly applied employee recognition programs demoralize employees and thus affecting their productivity				
There is no exact and no clear relationship between simple employee recognition programs and employee productivity				
Others (specify)				

Strategies of how M-Nic CRC can improve employee productivity through simple employee recognition programs

Please indicate by whether you strongly agree (4), or agree (3), or disagree (2), strongly disagree (1), in the statements where applicable.

9. The following are the strategies of how to improve employee productivity through simple employee recognition programs;	1	2	3	4
Deciding with employees what is to be achieved through employee recognition efforts				
Creation of goals and action plans for employee recognition programs				
Ensuring fairness, clarity, and consistency as they are important in employee recognition.				
Employee recognition approaches and content must also be inconsistent				
Being as specific as it can be, in telling the individual exactly why he/she is receiving the recognition				
Offering employee recognition as close to the recognizing event as possible.				
Others (specify)				